THE Questions Book

for Marriage Intimacy

Dennis & Barbara Rainey

QUESTAR
PUBLISHERS, INC.

THE QUESTIONS BOOK FOR MARRIAGE INTIMACY
© 1988 by Dennis and Barbara Rainey
Published by Questar Publishers, Inc.

Originally published as THE QUESTIONS BOOK—*Communicating Your Heart: A Great Marriage Builder*
©1985 by Dennis Rainey and Bobb Biehl

Printed in the United States of America

ISBN 0-945564-00-7

The authors and publishers believe so strongly in the value of these pages that we offer this guarantee: If this book doesn't improve
communication in your marriage and give you a better understanding of each other, we'll refund your purchase price.
Questions or requests may be directed to the Publishers at the address above. Refund requests must be accompanied by a sales receipt, and
must include a written statement that the reader has read the entire book and discussed the Thirty-one Questions (for at least twenty minutes
each) with his or her spouse, without learning more about each other and without any benefit of improved communication.

Acknowledgments

Bobb and Cheryl Biehl: You're at the top of the list of those who helped create this book. Your ability to ask the right questions is second to none. Thanks for your friendship and partnership in this book.

Donna Guirard: You are not only a great friend, but you have proved to be invaluable in taking dog-eared, messy manuscript pages and transforming them into a crisp, original product that strengthens marriages. Thanks for hanging in there with us.

Carol Spencer Morris: Your design and layout is the best. We appreciate you.

Lee Burrell: You are a tenacious production manager. Thanks for pushing this to completion. You are not only a great servant, but a faithful friend as well.

Jeff Tikson, Sue Stinson, and Elizabeth Reha: You comprise the best team a boss could ever hope to have. What a great bunch to work with toward our goal of strengthening marriages.

To OUR CHILDREN,
Ashley, Benjamin, Samuel, Rebecca, Deborah and Laura,
who give us joy.

To you we dedicate this book,
with the hope that each of you will experience a strong
and lasting marriage.

Yஂ OU'RE PROBABLY READING this book for one of two
very different reasons.

The first is that you and your spouse have a strong and loving
marriage, a relationship you so cherish that you want always to
be discovering new ways to support and enhance it. You
believe that anything this book can teach you about keeping
those communication lines open will only add further strength
to your marriage.

And you are right. Awaiting you here are many fresh
discoveries about your mate.

The other, quite different reason you may have picked up this
book is that the communication lines in your marriage are
frayed— perhaps even broken down completely. In fact, there
may be walls between you and your spouse, great gulfs of
alienation, formidable barriers to the open sharing you once
knew. You may be grasping desperately for help and counsel
that will show you how to rediscover each other, and to begin
communicating once again.

For you, too, there is hope in the pages ahead.

We share first with you the inspiring wisdom behind a great
secret for guaranteeing happiness in marriage. Then we show
you how to put this secret into practice in your marriage. Our
goal is to help you and your spouse grow together in oneness,
strengthening your marriage by strengthening your
communication. Please use all that is here
to enhance your life together.

*N*ow to begin: Imagine a hiking trip
in the Colorado Rockies . . .

*T*HE COLORADO AIR at higher altitudes is stimulating. It carries a fragrance of pine trees and wildflowers, and never completely loses the cold bite it gathers on its trip over the permanently snow-capped peaks. Even in midsummer you find it refreshing and encouraging as you ignore the beating sun and press ahead for another mile of backpacking.

The two of you are enthusiastic— if not rugged— explorers bent on finding forgotten trails and discovering new paths. You are two nature lovers off for a few days of solitude and personal communion with the great outdoors.

Except for each other you haven't seen a soul in three days, and that's fine. You couldn't imagine better companionship.

So it is that when rounding a trail bend on the fourth day out, you are amazed to see ahead of you a neatly preserved cottage cozily tucked in a thick grove of aspen.

You pause at first, seeing an elderly couple relaxing in a swing on the cottage's porch. Not meaning to disturb their serenity, you begin retreating as quietly as possible. But they notice you, and wave for you to come in for a visit.

*T*HEIR NAMES are Lee and Cora Donaldson, and they have summered for years in this secluded little cottage in the mountains. They haven't often met outsiders up here, and their openness and genuine pleasure at your arrival puts you at ease. You are soon sipping steamy tea and enjoying a plate of Cora's freshly baked biscuits.

With a friendliness still tempered by the natural reserve of strangers, you rave about the biscuits, ponder the afternoon

weather of the Rockies, and admire a deep blue lake that can be seen from the Donaldsons' rustic living room. But Lee and Cora are of that rare breed of people who quickly dispel any awkwardness of first meetings; before long you are all talking like old and comfortable friends— easily, seriously, with none of the verbal facades that characterize most new relationships.

*F*ROM THE BEGINNING it is obvious Lee and Cora have a special marriage. As they talk to you, they communicate with each other just as effectively with slight gestures and warm, knowing glances. In time the conversation drifts to the subject of their fifty-three years together.

Finally, warmed by the tea and encouraged by the friendship, one of you comes right out and asks the question both of you have been mulling over: "What's your secret? How have you been able to stay so happily married for so long?"

It's as though they were waiting for the question. They wink at each other, smile, and begin their story.

"*I*T BEGAN ON our honeymoon," Lee explains. "We had gone to Niagara Falls. We were on one of those tour boats that takes you through the mists of the Falls. Like a lot of young couples we were wrapped up in each other and thought the rest of the world had been put here for our personal enjoyment. We were watching other folks— older people, mostly— in that curious way young couples do. You know . . . we'd make up silly stories about folks, and wonder what they were thinking and saying to each other. Old age seems a million years away when you're young and in love."

Cora continues the story: "Two elderly couples on the boat particularly caught our attention. One couple was happy, even playful. But the other couple seemed preoccupied, depressed. They stood silently at the rail and didn't even seem to notice the Falls. Lee and I guessed that their marriage was probably like the boat trip: They had bought their tickets and planned to ride it out, but neither was getting much pleasure from it.

"Our suspicions were confirmed when we met the couple later while standing in the restaurant line at the lodge. The husband was a wealthy businessman from Indiana, and told us fondly about their comfortable house surrounded by beautiful grounds, into which the wife confessed having poured her time and energies. But later, when her husband stepped away for a few minutes, she seemed to read the sad questions in our minds. She confided that rather than sharing their home and its marvelous trappings, they merely coexisted under the same roof, emotionally isolated from each other. 'And I'm afraid,' she said, 'that we'll never change.' "

"While lying in bed that night," Lee adds, "Cora and I vowed to try never to end up like that. The problem, though, was that neither of us was quite sure how to avoid it. That couple from Indiana were probably just as happy and full of each other on their honeymoon as we now were. So why did they quit communicating? Or had they never started?

"Then we recalled the other elderly couple we had seen that day, as playful and fun-loving as school kids, whispering to each other, laughing, holding hands, and hugging each other. They had behaved more like newlyweds than Cora and I had.

We were amused by them, and even snickered a little, naively thinking— as young folks do— that love is reserved only for those under twenty-five.

"But after talking with the couple from Indiana, the other couple no longer seemed so silly. It suddenly became very important for us to meet them, though neither of us said so at the time.

"*F*INALLY, we did meet them— in the breakfast buffet line at the lodge, on our last day there. Looking back now, I guess it was just about the most fortunate day in all our years together."

"Those folks," Cora says with a smile, "were celebrating their fiftieth anniversary with a second honeymoon in the same place where they had taken their first. They owned a little flower shop in a Boston suburb. They had four sons and two daughters of their own, and had even adopted two neighbor children whose parents had been killed in a fire.

"They were so obviously full of life, and so in touch with each other— such a contrast to the other couple. So Lee and I had breakfast with them, and eventually asked them the same question you asked us: 'What's the secret?' And they told us. Every day for fifty years they had set aside at least twenty minutes strictly for talking to each other. Each day they talked out those little things that can become big things if nurtured by silence. Twenty minutes a day was their minimum daily requirement, sort of like a dose of vitamin C, but it wasn't their limit. They simply talked until the day's topics were talked out.

"After breakfast they gave us a sheet of paper with a list of

questions they often used to begin some of their daily sessions. They suggested we use the questions too, and urged us to make up new ones as well . . . a question a day for a lifetime.

"*THAT AFTERNOON*, Lee and I stood viewing the Falls a final time, and we promised each other that whatever pressures came into our lives, we would always follow the advice of the couple from Boston. We would always set aside at least twenty minutes a day to talk to each other.

"Since then we've missed our daily talks on only a handful of occasions. In good times and bad, when we felt fine or were as sick as dogs, when we had money to burn or were flat broke . . . we always *talked.*"

Lee points to a bell on the mantle. "We use that to signal the start of our daily conversation. We bought it at an antique shop on our way back from Niagara Falls. But it doesn't really matter whether you use a bell. Any couple can lay down their own procedures. What's important is to always find out exactly how the other person is feeling."

At this point in the conversation, Lee excuses himself and leaves the room, and Cora falls silent. Startled by the quiet, you realize only now how intently you've been listening.

Lee returns carrying a worn leather briefcase, which he opens on his lap when he is again seated. From it he pulls page after yellowed page of written questions and answers, the record of daily communication from their lifetime together. Scanning one page, then another and another, he and Cora select here and there a question and its answer to read aloud to you, occasionally with laughter, often with moistened eyes, and

always with the serene savor of fresh remembrance.

The questions are not complex, but from Lee and Cora's answers you realize how profoundly they call forth memories, longings, affirmations, commitments, shared perspectives— all the necessary thoughts and feelings for lasting happiness together. As Lee and Cora graciously share with you rich portions of their private past, the two of you find yourselves exchanging smiles and glances that say *I'd enjoy listening to you answer that question . . .* and *Remind me to tell you something very special I'm thinking . . . .* With a wink and a squeeze of each other's hands, you silently agree to begin the same habit of heart-sharing enjoyed by Lee and Cora— and, before them, the couple from Boston. As the lowering sun reminds you to rejoin the trail to find tonight's campsite before dark, Lee and Cora help you choose and write down thirty-one of the best questions from their long list— a month's worth of daily questions— to help you in a deep, new way to love and understand each other.

Here, now, are those thirty-one best questions. We encourage you to look them over together, as well as the suggestions on the next few pages for enhancing your times of sharing your heart. Select one new question to answer together each day, or as often as you can. It may seem a little awkward, but only at first. You'll soon be eager and ready to formulate questions of your own . . . and to share your discovery with other couples, as Lee and Cora did.

The Right Setting

Don't underestimate the importance of the when and where of your sharing times together. Be creative. Try establishing a personal, private, special meeting place.

Try to take twenty minutes for each question, just for the two of you. And don't rush . . . silence is okay.

Some ideas:

• Take an early-morning or late-afternoon walk together. Walk, talk, and share your answers together as a couple.

• Agree on a morning or evening sharing time together in the living room, and talk over a cup of hot tea or coffee.

• Meet somewhere for a lunch date, with plenty of time to go over a couple of questions.

• Take a weekend away to talk— we recommend two nights away from all distractions. We've especially enjoyed just randomly picking a number between one and thirty-one, then turning to that question and answering it. But it's just as meaningful to look through the book and select the questions that are most appproriate for now.

• A roaring fire in the fireplace always makes a great conversational setting. Why not toss a couple of pillows on the floor, grab this book and two cups of hot cider, and enjoy the warmth together as you begin sharing?

What to Write

As you go through the questions, write down your answers and date them. You'll find that the questions retain their relevance a year or five years or twenty-five years from now,

and you'll always find it interesting to look back and see how you answered them at different times in your life.

Write down words your mate uses frequently that tell you most about his or her feelings.

As you listen to and learn more about your mate, write down words of encouragement and praise.

Write down additional questions that come to mind during your time together. (We've included two pages near the back of this book to list some of your "best" questions.)

You can take turns writing— the husband recording his wife's responses on "Her" page while she is speaking, then vice versa. Or perhaps one of you likes taking notes better than the other, and can write down answers for both of you.

The Right Attitude

Listen . . . and look each other in the eye as you share and talk together.

Listen . . . and seek above all else to understand your mate.

Listen . . . and rephrase your mate's answers when appropriate.

Listen . . . and don't retreat when it feels uncomfortable. Share what's really important.

Listen . . . and try not to defend yourself. Remember, "winning" is not the goal. Understanding is.

Listen . . . and don't react negatively to your mate's answers. Instead, praise and encourage. Draw out each other's deepest feelings with further questions.

*Now turn the page to continue
one of the greatest adventures of your life:
Discovering one another . . .*

1

If you could keep
just one memory (of some past event
or period of time) . . . which would you keep?
Why?

_____

_____

_____

_____

_____

_____

_____

_____

_____

_____

_____

H I S

1

If *you could keep*
just one memory (of some past event
or period of time) . . . which would you keep?
Why?

_____

_____

_____

_____

_____

_____

_____

_____

_____

_____

_____

H   E   R   S

*W*hat do you think have been
the three most romantic times we've had together?
What made these times so special?
How can we keep the romantic side of our marriage
alive and exciting?

_____

_____

_____

_____

_____

_____

_____

_____

_____

_____

_____

_____

H I S

What do you think have been
the three most romantic times we've had together?
What made these times so special?
How can we keep the romantic side of our marriage
alive and exciting?

_____

_____

_____

_____

_____

_____

_____

_____

_____

_____

_____

_____

H E R S

3

*W*hat do you think have been the five
most important milestones we've passed together?
Why was each so important to you?
(You may want to list a lot more than five . . .
pleasant memories are fun!)

_____

_____

_____

_____

_____

_____

_____

_____

_____

_____

_____

_____

H I S

3

*W*hat do you think have been the five
most important milestones we've passed together?
Why was each so important to you?
(You may want to list a lot more than five . . .
pleasant memories are fun!)

_____

_____

_____

_____

_____

_____

_____

_____

_____

_____

_____

_____

H E R S

4

*I*n what single way
would you most like to see me
grow personally in the next twelve months?

_____

_____

_____

_____

_____

_____

_____

_____

_____

_____

_____

_____

_____

H I S

4

In what single way would you most like to see me grow personally in the next twelve months?

_____

_____

_____

_____

_____

_____

_____

_____

_____

_____

_____

_____

_____

H E R S

*W*hat two or three problems, if solved,
would make the most positive difference
in our marriage and family?

_____

_____

_____

_____

_____

_____

_____

_____

_____

_____

_____

_____

H I S

5

*W*hat two or three problems, if solved,
would make the most positive difference
in our marriage and family?

_____

_____

_____

_____

_____

_____

_____

_____

_____

_____

_____

_____

H E R S

6

*W*hat do you see as the three most important
decisions we need to make in the next year?
Why are they important? Toward what choices are
you leaning in each area? What would help us most
to make each decision wisely?

_____

_____

_____

_____

_____

_____

_____

_____

_____

_____

_____

_____

H I S

6

What do you see as the three most important
decisions we need to make in the next year?
Why are they important? Toward what choices are
you leaning in each area? What would help us most
to make each decision wisely?

H E R S

7

*H*ow would you describe . . .
  your ideal day (sunup to sundown)?
  your ideal evening?
  your ideal weekend?
  your ideal vacation?

_____

_____

_____

_____

_____

_____

_____

_____

_____

_____

_____

_____

H I S

*H*ow would you describe . . .
    your ideal day (sunup to sundown)?
    your ideal evening?
    your ideal weekend?
    your ideal vacation?

H E R S

8

*If you could spend
one uninterrupted hour today with
any person alive, who would it be?
What would you do or discuss?
Why?*

_____

_____

_____

_____

_____

_____

_____

_____

_____

_____

_____

_____

H I S

8

*If you could spend
one uninterrupted hour today with
any person alive, who would it be?
What would you do or discuss?
Why?*

HERS

9

*I*n what three specific ways
could we improve our everyday communications?
Where are we strong in our communications?
Where do we hit snags?

_____

_____

_____

_____

_____

_____

_____

_____

_____

_____

_____

H I S

9

*In what three specific ways
could we improve our everyday communications?
Where are we strong in our communications?
Where do we hit snags?*

H E R S

If you knew you had just six more months to live, how would you spend them?
What would you do?
Where would you want to go?

_____

_____

_____

_____

_____

_____

_____

_____

_____

_____

_____

_____

H I S

10

*If you knew you had just six more
months to live, how would you spend them?
What would you do?
Where would you want to go?*

_____

_____

_____

_____

_____

_____

_____

_____

_____

_____

_____

_____

H E R S

11

*What three needs in the world
trouble you most . . . the kinds of things
about which you say to yourself,
"Something must be done about this"?*

_____

_____

_____

_____

_____

_____

_____

_____

_____

_____

_____

_____

H   I   S

11

What three needs in the world
trouble you most . . . the kinds of things
about which you say to yourself,
"Something must be done about this"?

_____

_____

_____

_____

_____

_____

_____

_____

_____

H E R S

*W*hat specific part of
your work responsibilities do you find
most fulfilling? What part do you find
most frustrating?

_____

_____

_____

_____

_____

_____

_____

_____

_____

_____

_____

_____

H I S

12

*W*hat specific part of
your work responsibilities do you find
most fulfilling? What part do you find
most frustrating?

_____

_____

_____

_____

_____

_____

_____

_____

_____

_____

_____

_____

H E R S

*In your opinion, what three things
produce the most stress in our lives?
In our marriage? In our family?
What is your greatest area of stress right now?
How can we overcome it?*

_____

_____

_____

_____

_____

_____

_____

_____

_____

_____

_____

_____

_____

H   I   S

*I*n your opinion, what three things
produce the most stress in our lives?
In our marriage? In our family?
What is your greatest area of stress right now?
How can we overcome it?

_____

_____

_____

_____

_____

_____

_____

_____

_____

_____

_____

H E R S

*W*hat pops into your mind in each of these areas?
Your best day ever . . . Your most cherished gift . . .
Your most meaningful compliment . . .
Your best job . . .Your favorite relative . . .
Your favorite toy as a child . . .

_____

_____

_____

_____

_____

_____

_____

_____

_____

_____

_____

_____

H I S

*W*hat pops into your mind in each of these areas?
Your best day ever . . . Your most cherished gift . . .
Your most meaningful compliment . . .
Your best job . . . Your favorite relative . . .
Your favorite toy as a child . . .

_____

_____

_____

_____

_____

_____

_____

_____

_____

_____

_____

_____

H E R S

15

*W*hat dreams have you thrown away
(or kept secret) because no one encouraged you
to "try it," or because you feared you would fail?
If you could do anything in the world (and be
certain of success), what would you do?

H I S

15

What dreams have you thrown away (or kept secret) because no one encouraged you to "try it," or because you feared you would fail? If you could do anything in the world (and be certain of success), what would you do?

H E R S

16

If we became richer
than either of us could imagine today,
what would you like to do with the money?

_____

_____

_____

_____

_____

_____

_____

_____

_____

_____

_____

_____

H I S

16

*If we became richer
than either of us could imagine today,
what would you like to do with the money?*

_____

_____

_____

_____

_____

_____

_____

_____

_____

_____

_____

H E R S

17

*W*hat's heavy on your shoulders?
Where do you feel you're "going under"?
Is there any way I can help?
How can I make your life easier or better?
How can I help you really _win_ in life?

_____

_____

_____

_____

_____

_____

_____

_____

_____

_____

_____

_____

H I S

17

*W*hat's heavy on your shoulders?
Where do you feel you're "going under"?
Is there any way I can help?
How can I make your life easier or better?
How can I help you really <u>win</u> in life?

_____

_____

_____

_____

_____

_____

_____

_____

_____

_____

H E R S

*W*hat do you see
as my three greatest strengths?
How do my strengths complement yours?

_____

_____

_____

_____

_____

_____

_____

_____

_____

_____

_____

_____

H I S

18

*W*hat do you see
as my three greatest strengths?
How do my strengths complement yours?

_____

_____

_____

_____

_____

_____

_____

_____

_____

_____

_____

H E R S

*If you were suddenly removed from me
by something unexpected (such as death),
from what people would you most want me to seek
comfort and help? Whose counsel would you most
want me to avoid? Why in each case?*

_____

_____

_____

_____

_____

_____

_____

_____

_____

_____

_____

_____

H I S

19

If you were suddenly removed from me
by something unexpected (such as death),
from what people would you most want me to seek
comfort and help? Whose counsel would you most
want me to avoid? Why in each case?

_____

_____

_____

_____

_____

_____

_____

_____

_____

_____

_____

H E R S

20

What do you consider the three most important things we could do with each of our children in the next year? What are the three most important values we want to teach our children before they reach adulthood?

_____

_____

_____

_____

_____

_____

_____

_____

_____

_____

_____

_____

H I S

*W*hat do you consider the three most important things we could do with each of our children in the next year? What are the three most important values we want to teach our children before they reach adulthood?

_____

_____

_____

_____

_____

_____

_____

_____

_____

_____

_____

_____

H E R S

21

*In what single area
do you most want to grow personally
in the next year? Why?
How can I help you?*

_____

_____

_____

_____

_____

_____

_____

_____

_____

_____

_____

H I S

In what single area
do you most want to grow personally
in the next year? Why?
How can I help you?

_____

_____

_____

_____

_____

_____

_____

_____

_____

_____

_____

_____

H E R S

22

If we were stranded alone on an island for a month, what one thing would you most like to discuss at great length? Why? Besides necessities of food, clothing, and shelter, what would you want most to have with you?

HIS

22

*If we were stranded alone on an island
for a month, what one thing would you
most like to discuss at great length? Why?
Besides necessities of food, clothing, and shelter,
what would you want most to have with you?*

_____

_____

_____

_____

_____

_____

_____

_____

_____

_____

_____

H E R S

23

*O*f all the people
you've known in your life,
which three do you most admire?
Why?

_____
_____
_____
_____
_____
_____
_____
_____
_____
_____
_____
_____

H I S

23

Of all the people
you've known in your life,
which three do you most admire?
Why?

_____

_____

_____

_____

_____

_____

_____

_____

_____

_____

_____

_____

H E R S

24

*W*ho are your three closest personal friends?
What do you enjoy most about each one?

_____

_____

_____

_____

_____

_____

_____

_____

_____

_____

_____

_____

H I S

24

*W*ho are your three closest personal friends?
What do you enjoy most about each one?

_____

_____

_____

_____

_____

_____

_____

_____

_____

_____

_____

_____

H E R S

*If our house caught on fire
(and everyone was safely out), what three things
would you most want to save?
Why?*

H I S

*If our house caught on fire
(and everyone was safely out), what three things
would you most want to save?
Why?*

_____

_____

_____

_____

_____

_____

_____

_____

_____

_____

_____

H E R S

26

*I*n your deepest heart of hearts,
*what questions would you most like me
to ask you? What would you like most
to ask me?*

H I S

*I*n your deepest heart of hearts, what questions would you most like me to ask you? What would you like most to ask me?

_____

_____

_____

_____

_____

_____

_____

_____

_____

_____

_____

H E R S

*Why do you think we
are still happily married
when so many people around us are
unhappily married or divorced?*

_____

_____

_____

_____

_____

_____

_____

_____

_____

_____

_____

_____

H I S

27

*W*hy do you think we
are still happily married
when so many people around us are
unhappily married or divorced?

H E R S

*W*hat do you enjoy most about our sex life?
How can I improve? What do you wish
I would or wouldn't do? What key to
"turning you on" might I have been missing?
What have I been getting A's in?

_____

_____

_____

_____

_____

_____

_____

_____

_____

_____

_____

_____

H I S

28

*W*hat do you enjoy most about our sex life?
How can I improve? What do you wish
I would or wouldn't do? What key to
"turning you on" might I have been missing?
What have I been getting A's in?

_____

_____

_____

_____

_____

_____

_____

_____

_____

_____

_____

_____

H E R S

When you pray, how do you imagine God?
How do you imagine heaven?
What is your view of the Bible's value
to our lives?

_____

_____

_____

_____

_____

_____

_____

_____

_____

_____

_____

_____

_____

H I S

29

*W*hen you pray, how do you imagine God?
How do you imagine heaven?
What is your view of the Bible's value
to our lives?

_____

_____

_____

_____

_____

_____

_____

_____

_____

_____

_____

H E R S

30

*W*hat would you want said about you
at your funeral? How would you want most
to be remembered? What impression would you
like people to have about your life's contribution?
Your character? Your family?

_____

_____

_____

_____

_____

_____

_____

_____

_____

_____

_____

_____

H I S

What would you want said about you at your funeral? How would you want most to be remembered? What impression would you like people to have about your life's contribution? Your character? Your family?

_____

_____

_____

_____

_____

_____

_____

_____

_____

_____

_____

_____

_____

H E R S

*D*escribe what you want your life
to be like at age 70 (or, if you're already 70,
at 80 or 90). What do you want our life together
to be like at that time? What steps should we take
today to get there?

_____

_____

_____

_____

_____

_____

_____

_____

_____

_____

_____

_____

_____

H I S

*D*escribe what you want your life
to be like at age 70 (or, if you're already 70,
at 80 or 90). What do you want our life together
to be like at that time? What steps should we take
today to get there?

_____

_____

_____

_____

_____

_____

_____

_____

_____

_____

_____

_____

H E R S

*H*ere's a place to start listing
your own best questions . . .

_____

_____

_____

_____

_____

_____

_____

_____

_____

_____

_____

_____

_____

_____

_____

From One of America's Top Homebuilders . . .

If your marriage has benefitted from *The Questions Book,* you can strengthen it further with a "weekend to remember" at a Family Life Conference sponsored by Family Ministry. This book is part of an outgrowth of more than a decade of helping families across the nation through these conferences. Dennis and Barbara speak at several of them each year. If you would like to receive information on an upcoming conference in your area, please provide the information requested in the box below.

Also from Family Ministry is *The Homebuilders Series,* a set of Bible study and discussion guides for use in small groups. They provide positive help— based on biblical, workable principles— to strengthen marriages and bring families closer together. Use the box below to indicate your interest in finding out more about these practical tools for building a distinctly Christian home.

Check below also to receive a free subscription to *My Soapbox,* a monthly news-letter from Dennis on a variety of topics relating to the family and Christian living. It's an excellent way to hear from the Raineys on a regular basis.

Please return your completed coupon to:

Family Ministry
Post Office Box 23840
Little Rock, Arkansas 72221-3840

TELL ME MORE!

I am interested in . . . *(Please check)*

❑   Family Life Conferences
❑   *The Homebuilder Series* (Bible studies for couples)
❑   *My Soapbox* (Dennis's monthly newsletter)

_____
Name

_____
Address

_____
City, State & Zip